With love we ourselves... wit its inspiration.

Anthony

NetteWorth Group | Oakland, California

www.withheldambition.com

Publisher's Note: This is a work of non-fiction and is a book of therapeutic journaled poetry written by Mr. Anthony M. Walker during his lengthy prison sentence.

Book Layout © 2017 BookDesignTemplates.com

Withheld Ambition/Anthony M. Walker -- 1st edition
ISBN 978-1-7331930-1-6

Contents

Dedicated to the memory of:

Johnnie Mae Walker

Marcellus Walker

Eula Michelle Walker

Marcia Denise Walker

Eula Blackburn

Marcus Walker

Jonathan Roy

David Allen Jr.

Suzette Coleman

Gordon Thornton

To all the people I lost during the true making of me,
thanks for adding to my life in ways
that only you could.

ANTHONY M. WALKER

(A.M. WALKER)

Introduction

Within every stage of my incarceration there have been hurdles, heartache, obstacles, and quite a few road-blocks. My learning process however painful, was constructed and formatted to bring the very best out of me at every individual level of my development.

With this book I have chosen a writing route that has no true description.

Inmates across America and abroad face so many different angles of pain due to the woes of imprisonment, and sometimes it's easy to think you know what's going on from a distance.

In 20 years I have lost almost my entire family to some kind of illness. From my mother dying at the early age of 37 from a heart attack, to my Grandmother passing away due to the complications of Alzheimer's Disease, and my Aunt and Grandfather both passing away from kidney failure.

During all of this, I have suffered 2 light strokes known as T.I.A.'s (Trans-Ischemic Attacks). I've been left to my own devices by anyone and everyone I assumed was a friend, ally, or support system.

Through it all I have somehow found a way to smile as I've been forced to take this solitary stroll amidst the dangerous conditions cultivated by my previous choices.

In this book, I have some poetry, motivational quotes, and deep thoughtful expressions that were all written within the years that transformed themselves into decades with me still in the prison system.

As I look back upon my life when I was free, I can see clearly the blind theories I imitated and I wonder, what would have become of me had I did this? Or had I done that? I'll never know.

What I do know is, inside the many secluded moments of my prison term there have been instances of anger, times of confusion and conflict, images of love, hints of joy and the thunderous blows of devastating loss after loss.

These are the things that have made up my...Withheld Ambition.

A.M. Walker

Acknowledgements

To my beautiful and very supportive Queen Shawn, thank you for taking the time to really know my heart baby, you're the greatest woman I've ever known. Without you pushing me and challenging me, this would never have been a reality. Thanks for choosing "US". UOE.

Swavell "Ausar", my brother, you have become irreplaceable as an ally and friend, from young thugs to grown men inside a very dark place. Thanks for the Foreword, I love you bro.

To all my brothers I love - Kasheem, we've come a long way. Cheese "W.K.", we're friends forever. Final, from rebelling to Peer Presenters WOW! Scrap God, stay you that's why I love you GTS. Macaveli Moosa, you are my lil bro forever you'll see. Strategy, I got us dude don't trip. Piankhi, keep that pen moving I love you bro PRC. Wazie, I love you cuz we on one. Neol-o-Duck, I never forget my true friends. Eddie Mac, I miss you Unc. MJ "FB", fitness brothers is a movement stay in it. Willie "Hood", thanks for keeping yo boy fresh love bro. STG you are an inspiration for me lil bro. Much love to F.E.B. 360 Chambobread.

To all the people that I met along the way, you know who you are, I really appreciate being treated like a human being, thanks for that.

For all my bros repping that PRC/SYTU lifestyle, always keep in mind what I said from the jump and that's to STEP YOUR THRONE UP! Thank you to my bro, William Lopez, Payaso, for the cover art inspiration, love bro.

A special shout out to all the people that held me down all these calendars, I never take it for granted. To Angie, Eric, and Big Ke-Ke Sutton I love y'all and all my true comrades and sisters that keep me in their hearts and prayers. If you close your eyes for one second you can almost imagine the first time you saw me standing on Pulaski.........look at me now.

A great man once told me "Anthony, don't just sit in there and workout your body, work your mind out too so you can become a mature man". So, thanks Uncle Bobby for encouraging me from the first year I came to prison...I love you Unc.

Three Queen Dedication

There were three women that raised me, my mother Marcia Denise Walker, my Grandmother Johnnie Mae Walker and my Aunt Eula Michelle Walker. My three Queens or my three mothers were a very eclectic, sometimes strange, but no doubt loving group of women.

I wish that you could have met these women but I'll try my best to give you a brief description that still has the flavor to satisfy your taste buds.

My mother Marcy had a nickname "Two Tons of Fun", and she was a big beautiful woman with an even larger heart. When she entered a room you knew she was at the party, at the barbeque, or on your block. She was only 16 years old when she gave birth to me but that didn't stop her from going to school and getting an appropriate education to provide me with the things that I needed as a growing boy. She wanted the best for me and also wanted me to strive for success no matter what. It is her upbeat and overly charismatic personality that she and I share.

She left this world with the knowledge of her only child on his way to serve 27 ½ years straight in prison. That pain of thinking my transgressions might have killed her haunts me off and on to this day, a pain I may never get over.

Where can I really start with my mentor, professor,

angel and awesomely caring grandmother Johnnie Mae? Well, I must say first that she is responsible for my extreme optimism and my ability to transcend above my current restrictions. She raised me to respect my elders and she taught me that hard work is the true essence of humility. The prodigal matriarch of the Walker clan, she saw the beauty in all people and exposed me to all walks of life and cultures. We went to almost every parade in the Chicago area when I was a young man. She would say, "We are all in this world together Anthony".

That piece of racial acceptance is why I can get along with the human race to this day. Right before she wasn't able to come visit me anymore because she had Alzheimer's, she told me that I didn't need her to move forward in this life and that I had everything I needed at that point to become the great man she always knew I would be. A few years later she too left this physical reality with her student still in prison.

My Aunt Eula was a true gem, Michelle was what we called her, but to me, she was my sister, aunt, best friend and mother all wrapped into one. I would tell her that she was my everything. She actually dropped out of high school at the time of my birth so that my mother Marcy could focus on her education since she was the one with a newborn. Such sacrifice and loyalty to those she loved that it often felt like she was blinded by her dedication to others. A portion of her that I too carry.

Michelle never had any biological children of her own so

I was hers to care after. She took me everywhere she went to the point that people in our neighborhood thought I was her son, but I wasn't. Back and forth on dialysis, she still made her pain seem futile to that of my plights in the prison system. Before I got my head on straight and started walking a more righteous path, she said to me in only her own way "Anthony, you ain't tired of this shit and living this way?!" Those stern words rattled me at my core and made me think about my future.

The last time I spoke to her on the phone before she passed away, it was this sound to her voice that stopped me dead in my tracks. She accepted the collect call and it was obvious that I had awakened her from a nap, all I could muster from my mouth was "I love you Shelly and I just called to say thank you for being in my life all these years". That was the last Queen I had left. She too faded from this planet with her son still in prison.

These are the women that shaped a large portion of who I am as a man. They say that a woman can't teach a boy how to become a man, and that does bear some truth, but these women took me as far as they could and allowed the unconditional love that they instilled in me to do the rest. I miss them and hope that this book makes them proud of their son.

Words About the Author

Traditionally, when you call someone a "character" where we're from, (the West and South side of Chicago), It's more often used as a slur. It can be used as a put down designed in hopes of exposing you to the people as one who bears watching as we say. It can almost be said that this turn of a phrase (commonly used in these marginalized communities) can take the appearance of a pseudo scarlet letter.

But what I mean when I say character when describing my brother Pharaoh (A.M. Walker) is the exact opposite. For example, if I was writing an autobiography on my life and times on this blue marble, Pharoah would be one of the most memorable and colorful characters I've ever had the privilege of befriending on this journey thus far.

One of the liveliest personalities, possessor of an infectious charisma that refuses to be denied access to your heart once you've had a chance to share a laugh with him. A wellspring of energy, of talent, of true leadership ability, and a character with an indomitable will.

These are the attributes of my brother Pharaoh and by the time that you finish devouring this book you'll wish that you had the same courtside seats to his world, to the game he kicks that I do.

The content of Withheld Ambition is similar to a Sun

finally reaching maturation and going supernova. The outward appearance is that the Sun has reached the end of its cycle and died, the reality is that it has now spread the seeds of life throughout the universe. Many individuals who were destined to come through the ghettos of North America feel as if they're forced to withhold their innermost aspirations in order to survive.

But when you embrace struggle like Pharaoh has, you're able to evolve and explode onto the world stage as who you were manifested to be. Through his prose and poetry he has found his voice and if you pay close enough attention and if you're honest with yourself, you just might see a glimpse of who you are or who you can be. But only if you're able to withstand taking a deeper look within.

The pages of this book reveal the soul and the humanity of a man once lost in the storm searching for the meaning of life. Between the lines of this book you'll find the hope and wisdom one has gained through deep concentration and reflection. Most importantly, in this book you'll find more than anything else is the nature, and the character of our living Pharaoh.

Expressed by his brother and friend –

Ausar Un Nefer Ra Akhu
commonly known as - Swavell Toliver

Foreword

You can do all the changing you desire and all the soul-searching you want as well. What does it matter if you are all alone?

The prison setting is a very, very dangerous one. It is one that causes a normal human being to succumb to certain frustrations he/she cannot control. When your every move is watched, ridiculed and scrutinized, it is hard to stay calm. You are often egged on to not stay calm and go off track. Most of the time this is done just to entertain other inmates.

How would you survive an attack of this caliber on your mind? It would take more years than I actually have left to describe this overall journey and experience. The pull on your sanity and civility is the strongest you could ever imagine. Nights and days run past you as years chase away your youth. The time spent in various activities from weight lifting, playing cards, chess and checkers is distracted time wasted.

After you spend your time getting all the schooling certificates, where will you get work upon release? If a person without a conviction with a college degree can't find a job, then where will felons find reasonable work after decades in prison?

There is not one thing in here that can help you get the time back you lost as a result of your imprisonment. Nothing and no one person can help you make it through a lengthy prison term. If you are not strong enough, then you'll perish mentally and spiritually in all aspects of the bid and sentence.

When you commit crime and get arrested there is a thing called the "Justice System". You have choices in how your case is handled, by a bench trial, by a jury trial or by a plea bargain /sentencing agreement. All of those things are set in place for justice to arrive at some point. Now fast forward to reality, I am serving a 60-year prison term for murder in the first degree. By jury trial I was found guilty and some would say that justice was served. But was it? How can I make changes under these conditions? Especially when I am treated like the same man that got locked up years ago.

In closing, this has been pieces of my soul written in a form that I have chosen to share with the public. I've had 2 decades to think about my mistakes and transgressions. Over time I have even found a sense of my own maturity using experiences from my past as guideposts. There are many of us out there and in here who have some of the most profound potential known to man, but it has the tendency to go overlooked because we groom the wrong side of our thinking.

My voice is but one, but maybe, just maybe I can be that one justifiable decibel of sound that trembles the part of your mind and emotions that cradles your concern and compassion. Even the smallest awakening can stir an entire nation, and I can only hope my words do not fall on deaf ears.

2004

2,746 days in | 8,203 days to release

*What greater deprivation is there
than the absence of love and concern?*

All journeys have starting points and beginnings. Well, here I am going into my 8th year in prison. By now, my mother had passed away and I was still struggling with the notion that my lengthy sentence may have given her the heart attack that killed her.

2004 would also be the last year I would see my grandmother alive; she had been diagnosed with Alzheimer's disease in 2002. I got myself shipped out of the prison that was close enough for visits with her. This would be yet another foolish choice that would haunt me and teach me all at the same time.

With a lot of the puzzle pieces scattered inside decades of pain, I'm trying to start from a place of cognition and consciousness.

The first poem is titled "Monument" after my grandparents' marriage and how I perceived their 48 year union to one another. A fitting beginning towards restructuring my ambition.

Foundations should always be built on love as one of the key strengthening elements, so we begin.

Monument

03.11.04 | 2,816 days in

Tantalizing radiance engulfs around a centerpiece of
    illuminating craftsmanship,
Heavenly manufactured with breathtaking features, smooth
    texture, and top of the line, state of the art interior.
Such beauty this statuesque figure possessed,
    I stood motionless,
Dare I utter a word? Or seem absurd?
    Out of place amongst Cleopatra's predecessor.

Valuing courage but still conjuring confidence,
    my introduction spewing words like lava,
Performing with accuracy and butterflies, the subject
    matter, more than explosive.

The metaphors clashed competitively, but never enough
    to conceal the lustful magnetism,
With the foundation laid, not for long construction
    was under way.

Now that the parables have penetrated precisely past
    a platonic perception,
This classy connection can capture comfort upon contact.

As these sensitive sensations surge simultaneously
    throughout our cerebellums,
It is without question, the legacy of this lengthy liaison
    will outlast our libidos and linger a lifetime labeled as love.

P'd Off

6/18/2004 | 2,915 days in

Picture me pitching these persuasive thoughts with my pen in my prime with passion, behind my slave name you hear discussion and for obvious reason it's pandemonium in any shape, form, or fashion.

Yeah, my vision is personal, but I personify the perpetual perilous atrocities that me and my panel have been placed up under, so I'll be the player turned patriot, pay close attention as I pass through these parables laying it down smooth as peanut butter.

Inside the penitentiary people perceive me and my kind as parasites yet they should pause that perception, let those persecuting thoughts perish cause inside this paperwork I'm proving there's a percentage of my peers with a sense of direction.

That's why I'm pencil whipping those pansies that attempted to politic against my persistence, had I have continued pistol-gripping I couldn't have partaken in putting these paragraphs on these pages digging in the membrane of my pecan to do what? Make a difference.

I'm not attempting to patronize you with a play on words, I don't parlay in that pleasure to achieve a peculiar sense of vengeance, this is just a particular pattern penned poetically to polish my skills and hopefully I'm piquing your interests.

So when they practice polarizing or plagiarizing what I hold precious it has predestined for them to preview this piece, they are only passengers amongst a ride of perfectly placed predicates, and they have been penalized for assuming that all I know, no they have been penalized for assuming that all WE know are the streets...and that's why I'm P'off.

10.24.04

3,043 days in

Impossible it is to penetrate my thoughts away from the malfunctions I observed from my past career choice,

I had become so distinguished in the demoniac dialogue of street dwellers, my family counterparts were reluctant to trusting my voice.

Far beyond humbling and neither could I rejoice, so I salivated in silence wishing I could savor the taste of my deceased mother's last words,

Relishing in those never forgotten adjectives I pondered the notion of being too naïve to accept punishment that may have been well deserved.

"Charisma exudes from your pores, therefore you will be misjudged" my mother said, still my efforts for change are only for the better,

With my optimism in sight I sealed the envelope but somehow I knew my sincerest syllables wouldn't achieve a return letter.

So much for positive results.

2006

3,477 days in | 7,472 days to release

*Truth cannot be heard when one
has grown accustomed to loving lies.*

Menard Correctional Center is located in town called Chester, Illinois. A maximum security prison 350 miles away from Chicago, the farthest I've ever been away from my family and away from Chicago for my entire life.

They called Menard "The Pit" because it was basically built inside a hole in the ground. This was a scary place because you could go to the yard and look up at cows staring back down at you. There was a slaughterhouse up on that hill, yet another stench added to the smell of miserable lifers.

While I was there a guy committed suicide by jumping off the top tier, this is a vision that will forever be plastered inside my memories. I remember talking to him briefly because I was sitting in my cell waiting for commissary, he was climbing the rails. I assumed he was a scaffolding cleaner/worker and they usually have a harness around their waist.

So, I turned around and asked him, "What are you doing?" his reply was, "I'm going to the top!". Thinking nothing of it, I turned around and kept watching T.V., Then I heard people screaming from upstairs, "Hey, don't do it!". By the time I ran to the front of the cell, his body came flying pass going to the ground floor at a speed I can't explain.

The loud thud from his body hitting concrete sent extreme shockwaves through the entire cellhouse, a sound you'll never forget. Why? Because this wasn't a fairytale and you know you saw that happen.

In 2006, I had my first of two separate mini-strokes (T.I.A. – Trans-Ischemic Attack). I was standing in my cell talking to my cellmate when all of a sudden as I bent down to get some snacks out of my box to share with him, it happened. My entire left side of my body went numb, I felt my tongue fall in my mouth; I was speaking gibberish.

Scared out of my mind, I lay there on the floor for almost a full minute but it felt like an eternity. My cellie jumped out of the bed and began hollering on the gallery for the officer.

When medical staff finally arrived the nurse asked me what was the issue and I told her what happened to me, she looked me right in the face and said, "Strokes don't happen on the left side of your body" and she walked away. I screamed down the gallery, "What the hell does that mean?!". Of course, I received no reply. The nurse never returned, no follow up and I wouldn't get anymore medical attention for that until I had another one in an entirely different facility.

This year in particular changed me forever. Prison was, and is very real, and I had to really focus on making it out of here healthy, in one piece physically and of sound mind and maturity psychologically.

09.01.06

3,720 days in

There is an echo within my emotions and a strong
heartbeat amongst my thoughts,
There's a steady controlled pulse alongside my
feelings and heavy breathing deep inside my faults.

There is an awkward silence inside my anxiety and
obnoxious laughter surrounding my depression,
There's a blanket of stupidity covering my pride
and premeditated uncertainty within my questions.

There is unseen paranoia haunting my serenity and
unbridled madness smothering the seeds of my intuition,
There's a spontaneous idiocy controlling my caution
Enabling the true me to come into fruition.

There is an explanation for my journey and it may not
be on the surface nor within the words above,
Then there's the enormous possibility that all problems
could be rendered with the insertion of love.

Only in my dreams.

09.10.06

The founding father of all the great oceans, rivers and lakes now has to travel across rugged terrain,
The unpleasant nature of his negligence plagues his very essence cause on the surface he seems simpleminded and plain.

His skin-tone and texture has been rejected on countless occasions creating speechless adversity,
On the plane of thought he's brilliant leaving the naysayers baffled and extremely against ethnic diversity.

Since in which the words I pitch are locked away with me inside a maximum security prison who will actually listen?
Will the mistakes of my past plant seeds of doubt and ultimately crush the chances of others sharing my vision?

With the sand of ancient Egypt in my palms mixed with the strength of my deceased mother coursing through my veins, I will eventually attain our stolen legacy,
Treading across those same oceans I founded, marching triumphantly through the civilizations I built, destroying circumstance and rearranging the outcome of our destiny...but for now it's just caged brilliance. Or is it?

11.13.06

3,793 days in

Time truly seemed expendable during my lost days of lust, greed and harshness,
Chasing scattered images of mastered illusions kept me occupied enough to lose weight and sleep.

Trusting my tainted intuition led me to savor the taste of irrational thoughts as if it was red wine,
The constant drinking from an empty well allowed me to feel whole surrounded by nothingness.

Doing everything I wanted to do fed my cravings to become a man of major accomplishments,
Doing these things unplanned prematurely proved just how deep in my adolescence I stood.

As I sped through this worthless lifestyle trampling over others with no remorse I catered to my delicate ego,
Crushing countless relationships assuming my presence alone was enough to attain eternal love and respect.

A true glass house I was, with a neverending arsenal of bricks in the form of awkward statements and misguided judgment,
As distraught and desolate I may have appeared, if you would have looked closer to my attire I honestly wore our love on my sleeve.
Arthington and Karlov.

2007

3,842 days in | 7,107 days to release

Don't just be aware of your surroundings physically,
but also be aware of those thoughts
that surround your mind.
That's what determines the outcome of your future.

The growth process is rough, especially when you've been shuffled through several maximum security prisons for almost a decade. This year was the first time that I've been shipped to a facility that wasn't a maximum security.

January 10. 2007 I was sent to Hill Correctional Center, A.K.A. Galesburg. Honestly, I wasn't ready at all.

Maximum security prisons are referred to commonly as "Behind the Wall" because of the huge walls that surround them. However long you're there you never see cars, the freeway, or even a parking lot. You are closed off out of society for real even as the years mount up you can physically feel that truth.

The rules of engagement are different in comparison to "Behind the Wall" and other facilities of lesser or lower security levels. My first month in Galesburg I had two fights because my aggression level was high, and the respect level is different as the security level decreases.

What should have been refreshing and a chance to get more time out of my cell became strange, harsh and unfamiliar. I needed to work on my tolerance and after being put in segregation for 90 days, obviously I need to work on my anger. By the end of this year I was transferred again to a prison called Pinckneyville Correctional center from Galesburg after 5 ½ months, this is where I really changed.

Something happened that woke me up and made me realize I should stop withholding my ambition. Quite frankly, I didn't think I was stifling myself until I reflected in this jail.

I had my second T.I. A. (Trans-Ischemic Attack, or mini-stroke). But this time it felt like my heart was about to explode, first time in my entire life I thought I would actually die before my time. I couldn't speak due to the pain in my chest so, I wrote down my Aunt's phone number and asked my cellmate at the time to call her for me with this message if I died, "Michelle, I'm sorry for all this nonsense I put you all through and please find it in your heart to forgive me". After writing that message I passed out.

When I woke up the next day still alive of course, I made a pact with myself to change my eating habits and my overall lifestyle. Ultimately, that near-death experience gave me something to think about, simply put, it grew me up.

02.10.07

3,882 days in

Reacting to an effect I caused as the erratic strokes of my
brush created life on the smooth canvas,
Sin and punishment are but a mere facet inside the boxes in
which they try to label, scar and brand us.

An open text for the public if one would stop to see the epic,
riveting thriller within my eyes,
As I've seen the dissolving consistency of morality
and young women gambling the treasure between their
thighs.

No warm embrace for the drug addicted baby who cries,
Just cold shoulders, judgment and deviance,
I even admit, as a teenager I dwelled in fantasy and
Obviously waited too long to practice my obedience.

If it is too late for us, then I would swallow my
Ambition and pray to the heavens to die instantly,
Pour my ashes amongst the jails and ghettoes, and
Hopefully through my words someone will remember me,
        Cause I came and went.

03.03.07

3,903 days in

Thought I really knew you,
　　would have bet my life on it...

You changed in character,
　　your actions were cruel, distant
　　and heartless.

Love vanished, silence entered.
　　Uncertainty became certain.
　　You were finally gone.

Forever hurts when you're still
　　alive to understand its meaning.

Yesterday felt better, even the idea
　　of tomorrow seemed promising.

I'm not sure how I'll finish the week
　　without you..........
it's a failure worth trying.

03.18.07

3,918 days in

    A periodic glimpse of dignity appears suddenly, only to be shunned by the existing climate of control and spontaneous hostility,

    Courtesy seems to have never entered the premises in this lifetime as a barrier of haste consumes every inch of my humility.

    Supposedly years removed from the days of separate but equal, but one can cut through the irrelevant tension, more is there,

    Often apologizing for waking up in the morning to tyrants Whose abusive laughter echoes as they decide what's fair.

    Daily demeaning procedures occur to further confirm the lack of free-will, forcing me to smile through obvious disdain,

    Past choices created the ambiance surrounding this place But is being treated like a human being too much to complain?

    My ability to comprehend and decipher only makes this entire situation more disturbing, that a cloud of adapting hatred exists

    That's why for all these reasons stated my emotions have been in constant conflict and turmoil due to the pain this environment inflicts.

Can anyone understand?

04.03.07
3,934 days in

Spanish speaking Africans, English speaking Chinese,
crowded streets full of Jamaican accented Vietnamese,
Draped in hip-hop apparel, images of a dusty groove
casts a watchful eye waving at the liquored-up onlookers.
American flags raised high inside an Iraqi mosque,
Clashing adulterers smile at the seductive destruction
from propaganda,
The goose has slain the gander, planting characteristic
Traits across the vulnerable grey matter of our domestic
pedestrians.
The surface is entrenched with the DNA of misled
comrades, true soldiers whose cause fell within the hands
of slander and misfortune.
Dreaming about living while driving in gridlocked traffic,
the aroma of a promising future doesn't break the strength
of my sinuses.
I stand in a room bigger than the galaxy, staring at the
Crumbling of my tormented existence laughing at nothing,
Passerby's ask questions, curious eyes try to read my mind,
but my thoughts are somewhere between Egypt and Tibet.
Attempt to find me.

04.04.07

A melancholy mist covers the newly born plants, as baby birds chirp to the harmony of the refreshing spring season,

An a.m. jogger sweats to the oldies inside her ipod, as she strides in a rhythm she finds herself smiling for no reason.

Childrens' laughter clutter the streets as they play, bicker and fuss their way to the buildings of proclaimed higher learning

These moments come and go in a rapid display, proving that even if you sit still life in this world is always turning.

Happy people step in the name of love, every song is their song, watching the currency increase on the stems of money trees,

Spinning and turning, twirling and whirling, the used-to-be designated driver has given in, grabbed a cognac and passed off the keys.

Celebrating the overcoming of tragic scenarios with the support of friends and family brings joy during all the in-betweens,

Overlooking negativity as you stand proud and triumphant taking in the wonderful events beginning in the spring.

Wish that I could smell the roses....

05.31.07

3,992 days in

Quiet enough to believe sound doesn't exist, closed doors capture the undertone of imbecilic dreams.

Disease, famine and undisturbed indifference are not closely considered but are crushed by moronic ambitions.

"The descendants of slaves become rap stars, ballplayers, successful business people or irritating cellmates" he said, as he stumbled out of the diner.

My eyes moist with regret glancing at the bum who lost his bowels unnoticeably as that same scent doubled with cheap liquor and loose cigarettes.

Foolish of me to desire my deserved destiny.
Listen to my constantly attacked confidence pick up the pieces.

Cohorting with competent beings that stand still from a cerebral level undermines my critiqued awareness.

Feeling like a foreigner in a realm that I at one point seemed to love to take strolls and much needed naps in,

Not sure if waking from that unconscious slumber was so much of a bright idea, but where do I go from here on?

Tears won't strengthen this movement, they will more than likely be labeled as a weakness and laughed at with a thousand chuckles.

But I assure the curious idle-chatterers that peace should be your forefront, cause within this circumference entails the legacy of endless strategies.

You think I should go back to sleep?

06.10.07

A still picture of illuminating features brought to
life inside my fantasies. Untainted in purity. Fresh and
surreal.
Everything shivered when our lips danced with one
another. Singing in the complex melody of eternity.

Dusk chased dawn. The warm coat the sun gave us made
me understand reality and destiny followed my footsteps.
As she stood before me I tried not to blink, missing
a second of her beauty would anger me.

Days became years, and I still recall the exact second
when I found love in the form of breathing flesh.
It would take me a million eternities to divulge my
praise and thanks, and even that seems impossible
but there's no obstacle I can't test...
with her I've gained momentum.

Nurtured Endeavors.

06.10.07

4,002 days in

A slight impulse of decimation pervaded my mind briefly.
No instruments handy to strum a catchy tune of redemption.
  Copied poses are meshed with the mistakes of an era once
relevant. Stopping to stare, my eyes hear the message.

  Vibrations within the airways corrupt the frequency,
now hearts around the globe flatline simultaneously,
  Only to be reincarnated as terrorists and plague the
planet with a thousand years of vicious plunder.

  An environment overtaken by any and everything except
valiant righteousness. Complacent inside hideous actions.
  A loud thump of bass explodes the silence only to
introduce the host of projectiles that came careening through
the hospital nursery.

  Generations of innocence lost, raised to inherit the
guilty pleasures of their ancestors' indulgences.
  The lighthouse shines the truth upon the sinful society,
but they use it to tan and to continue loading their clips
of hedonism and illusion.

With time, life becomes death.

06.25.07

Time waits for nothing that exists on this planet.
I release the filth that attempts to hover around my mind.
Daily I look to intercept from the ethers and atmosphere
a historical ideology.

Open wounds from life's reality infect my future with
the scars of hate and the cowardice of jealousy.
My desire to evolve is too strong and potent to be
superseded by the vortex of faithless dominance.

"Allah watches all" is the rough whisper the Pope hears
from his balcony as his empty wave touches no one.
The words of divine prophets have been twisted to
further ensure the legacy of the devil's retirement plan.
The souls of my family tree rests underneath my eyelids;
I dream of fire and see blood every night.
I can taste the last thoughts of the dead and innocent
slaves, optimistic in all their endeavors,
Using what I have to step on the visions that seem to
be so irrelevant to my peers.

Trying to chase time with an unlikely array of schemes
and outlandish plots. Dying to just make sense.
My mind breathes relative to a journal of epic and
unprecedented proportions, eternal with the galaxy's infinity.
I have a doctorate in making mistakes and have fully
attained my P.H.D. in bullshitting, but still the cornucopia of
my thoughts are statuesque in brilliance.

Or so it seems.

07.15.07

Can a strong sense of faith and optimism be nothing more than an illusion as well?

My intelligence is challenged to grasp quickly and decide which truth shall govern my existence.

I am waging a war within, fighting to yield the falsehoods that inhabit my surroundings daily.

More than one me fights. It is he who I wish to win that has the lesser chance at victory.

Pain has the supreme advantage of gained experience, while happiness mimics spring, coming only once a year.

My ascension from a ridiculed dimension has come and now I must transcend above the poisonous scrutiny of the world or be overtaken by blasphemous scavengers.

I might already be gone.

07.19.07

4,041 days in

For however brief the moment is I am right in the midst of a stranger's world.
Intertwined somewhere amongst their ambition and passion I rest by eardrum on every word.

Without an insecurity in sight they divulge the closest intimacies gathered in a lifetime,
sometimes small portions of pain and grief are alleviated with me being the source of release therapy.

I may never see a large percentage of them again, so I embrace the laughter and the stories quietly,
Relishing deep within the camaraderie of a short-lived friendship as if it were infinite.

I am but a fly on the wall, forced to eavesdrop on the Lives of those I'd rather not have met,
Yet, through these calendars in prison I have gained a Huge respect for my comprehension.
Hearing people in their rarest form.
Tender Vulnerability.

07.26.07

4,048 days in

Explain to me the wondrous works of the oceans,
rivers, peninsulas and the enchanting colors of the sky,
   Share with me the joyful inebriation of an Italian
vineyard compiled with a fresh loaf of garlic bread before
I die.

Dance hand in hand with me while on a Caribbean cruise
across the Atlantic, smiling non-stop to the Bahamas,
   Shower me with Revlon coated kisses on a Lufthansa
flight headed for Europe holding our love's promise.

Almost coughed up a kidney laughing so hard in Sydney
as we had a tour guide through Australia's beautiful outback,
   Running with the bulls in Spain was exhilarating but
our acrobatic trysts in London threw out my back.

As the darkness of night consumes the memories of
daylight among sporadic noises I can hear my heart beating
really hard,
   It's then within my jail cell I search for mail and
Realize that I'm living vicariously through postcards.

Next time I should take a few pictures.

08.12.07

4,065 days in

My life has been death after death as I've tried to calculate one breath after breath.
See to me it's simple, I died when I took that oath and turned my hat to the left.

Since then my only lasting memories are the images of a vicious courtroom shooter.
A hungry prosecutor, squeezing round after round of words at me like a chrome German Luger, receiving more time than you can add with a ruler.

Now I sit in a cramped little cell chasing my demise at a turtle's glance,
Wondering if I die in this lonely ass cell, will my enemies or my family dance?

The future can't offer me anything substantial that my soul doesn't already know.
And that's if the dirt of my teenage mind controls my past how can my adult brilliance get to glow?

I took too long to give a damn huh?

09.03.07

4,087 days in

Distressed.
Haunted.

Enclosed confines create no refreshing memories
to sample amidst peculiar specimens.

The future cradles before it the fragrance of
isolation and rejection.

A day in the life wouldn't justify or build the
story to the effect of which it must be grasped.

Left to perish in a habitat of excessive force,
intellectual regression, and mental abnormalities,
I find myself sprinting to a logical hypothesis as
to why my spirit declines retirement.

At this pace, how much tenacity can one muster to
Even complete this absurd race through life?

I may need a personal trainer.
Know any discounts?

09.28.07

4,112 days in

Scheming maneuvers have been intricately extinguished
Permeating growth, development and change.
Forsaken gestures diminished, elevated horizons unseen,
Slightly irrelevant and shadowed by darkness.

Gracious lovely founders of the foreseen phrases.
An eon of exaggerated gratitude will reign supreme.
Two gorgeous Grandparents, and always beautiful mother
and an extremely overprotective Aunt. LOVE.

With irrefutable strength and wisdom firmly grounded,
doubtful occurrences are frequent.
Oh, to surpass irregularity, bigotry and stupidity.
Days and nights should never imitate hell.

Images of Chicago's phenomenal skyline rests in those
memories of mine I'd pray not to ever forget.
It is caught in time I record the only thing I can
truly afford.........a piece of expression.

Now what?

11.07.07

4,152 days in

Burned emotions suffer on the plane of reality,
misguided common sense is conformed and molded to accept
the fatality of my individuality.
Time wasted.
Suspended inside a morbid galaxy of deceit.
Drifting aimlessly, shaking hands with walking death
as I converse with ignorance and embrace negativity,
Knowing love is brilliance refined yet, often dissolved
hearts seeking retribution in the land of anonymity.

The darkness of yesterday antagonizes the dreams of
tomorrow,
Crowded loneliness breaches the areas containing all
of my sorrow.
I have a lot to give still, I only feel hollow,
while truth and consequences have bottled the pride
it took me 11 years to swallow.
Do you have any rehabilitation I can borrow?
Engulfed.

11.11.07

4,156 days in

The allegiance of eternal contracts, severed not by
simplicity but indivisible amidst complexity.
Compared to nothing. A character of allure, the scent
of cultivation defined by courtesy.

A smile sculpted by saccharine edges. The deep layers
demand respect with eloquence.
No labels nor painter's canvas could convey in speech
or oil the message underneath.

Chapters of unscripted perfection. Even the twilight
would take a pause at such illumination.
Implemented devotion walks above adversity. The words
were chosen as time within the night stood still.

Conversing with elegance provides stimulation.
Heightened senses explored, navigated by experience.
The future is as unpredictable as the source and
origin of her beauty. Still, I am content with uncertainty.
Sometimes happiness doesn't come
with a map or any instructions.

12.06.07

4,181 days in

The beauty of strength in the struggle carefully
exposes the true powerlessness in muscle,
Doused in flames are the charred remains of prudent
wisdom collected during the tussle.

Partially paranoid yet mildly apathetic, just for
my own convenience I'll refrain from being apologetic,
Counting down days as my worth gets appraised chasing
food for thought amongst the anorexic.

Loose dialogue in noisy quarters reveals the deafening
Silence inside the boundaries of the cerebrum's borders,
How can one teach and uplift when he is only a shadow
behind his gift, who am I to give orders?

A falcon with broken wings can only picture the sky,
living a lie savoring images of gliding gracefully above
you and I,
The brilliant effort placed on the notion to try will mean
what to whom when we inevitably have to die?

Where's my legacy?

2008

4,207 days in / *6,742* days to release

———

Opening your mind to new thoughts, events,
and scenarios only proves that you are not suspended
in time, but you are always able to evolve.

———

When your eyes open up and you're able to see things in your life with true clarity, everything changes. How you handled all of your life's situations before is different, and you question every motive you've ever had. The conscious brothers in prison call it "seeing with your third eye" or waking up from an unconscious slumber.

In this year so many wild things were happening in the "free world" as well as in my world inside the prison. My grandmother, mentor, best friend and teacher all wrapped in one, passed away. It was final, Alzheimer's Disease took my Queen. For some weird reason you think that your family member is different and that they'll miraculously beat that debilitating disease.

Not having her for the years that lead up to her passing was scary within itself, but at least when I called sometimes she would still remember my name. I could hear her voice and for a brief minute I could trick myself into believing that she can make a fast recovery. Insert reality here: she was gone and now the student had to lace up his boots for real and somehow become the teacher, and more so, become a man.

Barrack Obama was running for President of the United States and he eventually won at the end of this year. A black man with the audacity to run for the highest office in the land made all of us on the inside take serious notice. I even wrote the poem on 4/29/08 about my feelings concerning the language against him on the campaign trail.

This was my 12th year in prison, I was still searching for an ideology to keep me centered, and I was praying to never become institutionalized or what I've called "socially unrecognizable". I just didn't want to get lost in here, it sure seems easy to do so.

01.16.08

4,222 days in

Annoyed by hideous laughter, entrenched and enveloped
between a low vibrational octave and death.
Punctuated pugilism promotes my plights, describes the
stains on my heart, gathering the worthy remnants of
what's left.

Spewed ruthlessness stimulates the psyche of the
unconscious instigators, incompetent yet tranquil among
that stupidity.
Walking proudly, dancing on the bones of those who
died not knowing, while hallucinogenic drugs attract
life's humidity.

Lucid facts expose the one-dimensional, being the result
and not the cause has proven darkness is damaging,
When disparaging comments transform into self-esteem
and intelligent dialogue, that's when it's time to
start panicking.

Or is that time
already here?

02.04.08

4,241 days in

    Flushed into a gaping razor-edged portal,
bleeding from the severe cuts still feeling no pain.
    The remainder of the once joy-filled moments fizzle
out like a candle trying to shine around the stars.

    Days have become galaxies, while years have
turned into eons and tomorrow still seems promising.
    Secretive prisms reveal the ingredients that are
used to create the salty taste of teardrops.

    Gathering wood to keep that eternal fire going
feels useless around those who love it bitter cold,
    My pulse tangos and cha-cha's to the music that
the flatliners get lost in.

    I have learned to compose my own symphonies,
so the tunes I hear will be the sounds I like.
    Now I can dance the night away laughing,
satisfied with the orchestra that I orchestrated.

                I've chosen to live...
                    It's a difference.

03.13.08

4,279 days in

Still frames.
      Sad portraits.
Complaining corpses,
geniuses of the underworld
where darkness brightens
death.

Dissolved intent.
      Exhausted enthusiasm.
When did preparing to be
embalmed become so fashionable?
I never received the memo.

Practicing mental telepathy
seems realistic since written
or verbal expression continues
to fail.

Nowadays the crows' feet pupils
Stare us down and only deliver
Destruction.
What can we do to distract those
deceased principles from
consuming us?

Smelling the thought of us proudly
claiming ourselves as products of
an experimental environment
rumbles my bowels like a worthy
laxative.

      We've all grown fond of this.
      Identity Crisis.

03.20.08

4,286 days in

Uncomfortable.
    Pleased closer to disaster.
The aftermath of lonely hearts are grim discoveries
of ruthless darkness unkempt.

A fortress of despair, built on quicksand and
landscaped by novices.

Untouched truth lives at that infinite corner on
the top floor of eternity where such feeble limitations
of thought doesn't reside.

Aimless royalty fathom only the dregs of scorn
ideals.
The direction of misguided expression confuses
the rhythm of unforeseen desires.
        Innocence devoured.
        The American Way...Bravo|

04.05.08

4,302 days in

Fond of the pleasure exploration.
  Satisfied touches make fingertips
    Something worth having.

Inside lengthy trysts lies the expended
  dedication of two forces combining to
    create combustible ecstasy.

Before the long-awaited release of fervent
  captivity rests a calm utopia.
During the violently joy filled liberation
  of contributed efforts,
  the journey seems and feels unmatched
  and without explanations.

Fond of the pleasure exploration.
  Above and beyond, and nowhere to be
  found best describes my attempt to make
  sense out of how loving your company feels.

WOMEN......without them I am without.

04.12.08

Searching for diversification, seeking the expected
elevation only with no avail.
Doors of mental capacities open to evolve by the
confidence of the key holder.

Drama. Conflict. Turmoil. Betrayal.
Unseen and unknowingly. A conscious fighter has to
crush the manacles of struggle.

Defeat has its strengths, if in between the agony
of the loss, experience claims the appropriate force
of being a virtue.

Moderate tenacity is the reality of lifeless hosts
chasing half-hearted results.
Loaded burdens are appointed to the chosen patrons
of destiny and wordless conviction.

Land mines are seemingly strategically placed in
the pathway of the survivors, attempting to deter
progress made.
This beautiful contradictory we call life has survivors,
victims and inhabitants.

Some of us are just here.

04.20.08

4,317 days in

Chastised forever
inside the
shadows of seditious
behavior
Enticed still
by the emptiness
of aimless
distractions
I liberate my
thoughts
on the basis of
narrow findings
in truth
where empathy
should live
notwithstanding
ridicule.

Intrinsic ideals.

04.29.08

4,326 days in

Perusing footnotes inside graphic novels,
expecting to respect ideas within a brief overture.
Contaminated moralities evoke the pure in heart,
removing critical bandages of harsh wounds.

As seasons change, a climate that has resonated
amongst some startles the weatherman.

Illusions of grandeur mixed in all my drinks,
One must honor and admire the secret tyranny,
Exquisite vandals have smeared graffiti on all
untainted visions of beauty.

Intimately soothed by governing apprentices of
disaster; a higher seduction, how awesome!
Bathe me in atrocity, moisturize me with slander
and clothe me in despair.

I'll still look good.

05.14.08

4,341 days in

Unused encouragement waits alongside the rough edges
of torment and vulnerability.

The scorching pavement away from experienced failures
has left an arsenal of blisters, filled with all the
aromas of lost battles.

Measuring the volume inside this agony defeats
tomorrow's purposes while commemorating those historical
mistakes made in sedation.

Worn out but rather vibrant. The strange chemical mixes
simultaneously with large doses of unexplainable solutions.

Out of the abyss smeared in obvious unworthiness rose
splendor, misplaced luminescence, keen nobility all carved
in approachable extravagance.

Polishing new jewels and shining royal ornaments has
cleared the aisle where project stricken rituals once
took place.

Divine luster resurrected.

05.20.08

The formula for destruction are one in the same with the
ingredients of seduction
trapped in the belief of worthy goals, exclusive moments
breeze pass my coupe that runs on molasses

Street jargon is the means by which I often create
beautiful illustrations of naught and pleasure
certain scents ignite a nostalgic atmosphere throughout
the savings account known as my memory bank

Circling the atlas in one day. Surfing the Milky Way
singing love songs to the inhabitants of Venus
applauding the ears that fell in my hands, whispering
hope, screaming love and laughing faith

Sand in my pocket from previous expeditions allows
me to consume the visions of trampled beginnings
sordid dreams are merely appetizers to those who have
disastrous realities as their main course

Passages lined with the insolation of triumph are the
garments my adjectives dress to impress in
legendary pronouns exceed the plateau battling victory
and settle on the island of greatness

Prognosis-Survival
Someone has to.

06.18.08

4,376 days in

Desecrated armor covering a damaged spirit,
loud chants shake the balancing act of life.
Messages of melancholy are embroidered on the
souls of the earth's offspring.

Silence only caters to the lasting effect that
ignorance brings at the break of dawn.
Disturbing him isn't an inconvenience but more
like a mission for the restless.

Precious zombies of unused excellence make
repeated attempts at grasping liquids,
The notion alone is wrapped in absurdity yet,
Highly logical to the illogical.

The stumbled disaster of constant association
has become a disease that chips away more armor.
In the shadowy distance the blur of revived
greatness is resuscitated...flatlining and almost
gone...but still here.

Juggling life is a mission when
you live at the circus.
Peanuts.

07.24.08

4,412 days in

Caught or held in dangling suspense are the
Conceived authentic discussions.
Moments of greatness.
Gratification without touch,

One locked stare can change days of isolation
into confident overtures of harmony and misplaced
aggression.

Certain voices that reach beyond the physical
manifestations have the drive to awaken the soul's
alertness.

We seek clarity within these earthly connections,
finding shelter in the company of passing laughter and
building pain on the torrid bridges of adversity.

More than a specified emotion can define best
describes the complicated energy surrounding the
craving to be needed.

Sublime auras...I need you.

08.09.08

4,428 days in

    Visually sketching these moments moves the
bittersweet liquid drops across my face.
    Unbeknownst courtesy and compassion that
never reaches broken hearts, console lonely
particles in the land of nowhere.

    Let whatever happens happen to those doves,
if the sound of their tears creates melodious hymns,
my sorrow surely arouses enchanting ballads.
    Serenading the fallen soldiers with empty
dreams of having it all,
    Only to wake in the middle of what's left
to realize I may have missed the call.

What if the phone never rung?

09.09.08

4,459 days in

   Gaps inside growth bombard sessions of peace only to
Shower the arena with portions of hypocrisy...self-imposed.

   Many moons shuttle pass my visual, the night breeze
cascades through my cell window...I vaguely remember
freedom.

   Days elude certain areas of my once tainted
conceptualizations, while the nights are filled with optimistic
plans for the future...a riddle written in what seems to be
invisible ink.

  How much time has to pass in prison for me to be considered
a person that threw way an entire lifetime?

          Maybe I just answered the question.
              Beyond language.

09.11.08

4,461 days in

One destroyed barrier has appealed
      to a mysterious form in space.
To fathom unlearned intent strains
      the different variables attainable.

Portions of an unknown characteristic
      cannot be placed into words,
The race has been run, the training
      for the marathon never ends.

Even consumption too heavily of your
      favorite food can cause you strife,
If you never knew what favorite stood for
      would you still over-indulge?

A capsule maybe, a vessel sometimes,
      but a BEING forever.
As I float within, I float within a planet
      that floats within SPACE.
That space floats within an eternity.

           So, what are my individual
           limits?

09.27.08

For days I missed sleep contemplating
what words I could possibly utter.
What metaphors, paraphrases and verbs
could I conceive to not lose my old lover?

Seems like once again my past has
found a way to bring me to tears,
Constant opportunities lost at real love
cause I'm still facing many years.

The formula I use to express myself is
all I have to get all my points across,
In my cell I hope that this same formula
doesn't create a devastating loss.

Many times I have allowed where I am
to hold my feelings under my breath,
So with this I figured I'd say, "I'll forever
love you." just in case it's the last chance
I had left.

       If I could only turn
          back calendars...but I can't.

10.16.08

4,496 days in

    Invisibility smothered in naked coverings,
absurd light bulbs are cast out, shunned and
ridiculed.

    A subtle murmur contains small vibrations,
not enough decibels to muster up the appropriate
sound needed and undoubtedly desired.

    Hesitation seems to be working out nowadays
cause I can feel it's strength inside what are
supposed to be close knit connections.

    Enthusiastic masculinity becomes weathered
down and some begin to dress themselves in failure
and denial.

    In the winter I heard they are draped in blankets
of inadequacy.

11.09.08

4,520 days in

Parading inside the midnight chapter,
days become a sequel to pessimistic personas
Indecisive cliché's shrugged off as bad
omens hold substance in the underworld.

Walking tombs with shattered dreams
awaken to the loud chants of blasphemy,
deceit and hypocrisy.
Being serenaded by fallacy must be
nicer than the reality that truth brings.

Divided and separated, removed and torn
apart. The harsh symbolism of a fate so
grueling needs a taste of illumination.

Despite the denigration I tend to
camouflage my tears with laughter, wrapping
my fears in hope knowing that one of these
days...one of these days.

Or I'll just expire before
that day arrives.

Good Life

12.10.08 | 4,551 days in

Attracted to infinity, sobered minds
dwindle between cognition and insanity.
Disenfranchised spirits lie dormant,
minorly miserable distracted by degrading
circumstances of isolation.

Irritable contemplation, thoughts of
mediocre mistakes play hauntingly through
a single day in assisted captivity.

Incentive for positive escalation in
deeds live on the top floor of trust,
correlation and optimism.
Neither of which live in my world.

Countless souls perish, never getting
another chance to flourish and really know love.
Since balance entails room for all occurrences,
then this must be the good life.
Does circumstance trump brilliance?

12.20.08

4,561 days in

    On the street where complexity intercedes with
Perplexity is an enigmatic residence,
    Bruised egos and poor self-images deprive what
Cannot be translated.

    In a state of order disarray finds comfort and
Madness feels bearable.

    Crowded buses and subway cars, walking an
Eternity on an infinite path.
    Home never existed, laughs were very much artificial.

        Fabricated realities.
        Designed dimensions.
        Who created fitting in?

12.27.08

Kamikaze reigned on the quiet souls,
days were bleak but all what they should have been.
Selfless angels dance to the seductive cadence
of gunfire and unheard screams.
The dawn before, luminescent, joyous, dependable
and safe.

Anger showers upon truth with a thunderous
blow tailored in opinion,
Hastily, pride is consumed by a mistake etched out
in the divinity of destiny.

The same place kamikaze reigned, harmony had once
sung hymns and created heroes,
With patience voiceless and seemingly devoured,
defeat gains prominence.

Loyalty,
Strength,
Timeless.
A wrist with no watch.

2009

4,573 days in | 6,376 days to release

———

Believing in something or someone
doesn't make you weak or naïve.
This is your optimism saying you have faith that
in time something positive will happen.

———

After all that hope in closing 2008, I still felt like Luke Skywalker when Yoda died, I was in the midst of my Jedi training and my mentor suddenly passes. I had to find my way through this life inside all of my dilemmas without the wise counsel of my Granny to guide me. Finding my way with 17 more years left on my sentence was rough, I had to find inspiration out of thin air.

Capturing the essence of my pain and putting it on paper in the rawest form possible was the only way to successfully move through dangerous prisons and stay sane.

Death seemed to surround me. Not only was my family dying one at a time, but my homies were being murdered on the streets at an alarming rate. Made me believe that I would have been a target as well had I remained free.

I grew accustomed to taking losses, I felt like winning for me was staying alive and surviving this sentence. I had to search my soul for a reason to care, to carry on, and to not destroy myself or destroy everything I encountered.

Making adolescent choices like being in the streets and joining a gang organization came with some serious adult consequences I never saw coming. This may have been the year I began smiling at myself in the mirror for motivational purposes. After brushing my teeth, I would look directly in my own eyes in the mirror and smile at myself.

My hope: that the release of those endorphins could help me survive just one more day. Especially when days become decades at the pace of a snail running a 5K. "I need to make it" had become the mantra I said to myself anytime things got mildly overwhelming. Indeed, I would make it, time was proving that. I wasn't "just surviving," I was thriving amidst the B.S. and hoping Yoda was proud.

03.03.09

4,634 days in

Standard.
    Repetitive.
        Fantasy permeates language barriers.
    Heartless, mindless vessels roam eternally.
    That road is fascinating in a "kill me now"
        sort of way.

        Diabolical ignorance suffocates the foolhardy
          who admire wisdom,
        Why search when every crevice has been dominated
          by such blatant emptiness?

        Guilty pleasures are systematically tallied
          in the silence of my cowardly motives that
          still strangle chances for change.

            To finally give up is
            something worth wondering
            about...selfishly.

05.20.09

4,712 days in

Disappear,
    behind the obvious but seen
    trampling over obscurity.
    Small layers of a surface
    entangled by founded moralities
    carve lanes that seem to mock
    the origin of causalities.
Disappear,
    in the methodical tackle box
    of scapegoated bait
    left to be reused over, and
    over, and over until depletion.
Disappear,
    inside loose language uttered
    from spiteful opinionated
    caverns.
Disappearing from reality,
    drifting in cave-like fixtures
    where hate, despair and
    uncertainty preside over the
    unlikely taste of pleasant
    encounters.
Disappear?
    I have.
    I am lost of the world.
    To many I have disappeared.
    To millions I don't exist.
    To some I never have.
    How can I disappear if I was
    never seen?

07.08.09

4,761 days in

Another part of me
obsolete to the
untrained
Visualizing the
delicious taste of
caramel
Bittersweet apple
all lonely
fallen so far from
the tree
Resiliency shaken
at the root by
mammoth inquiries
A true sign of
times caged so
perfectly between
the lines
Outside the lines
the teardrop-stained
legacy is programmed
and controlled
Left to quarrel
with the hellfighters
which force will
prevail?
Am I chosen or
simply a person who
makes choices?
Certainly a few
choice words will help
make a decision.
Parallel but crooked.

07.15.09

Genuinely I had thoughts of
reclaiming your allegiance
to my once important spirit
and features.

The audacity of me
to foolishly think words
are enough to win a better
place inside your mind.

Controversies and documented
doubts have maintained
a strong hold on your heart,
that typical pattern of
distrust and guarded emotion,
I am mindful of its existence.

Should I subject myself to
further silence
allowing human frailties to
control the notion of optimism?
There is a one-sided position
taken in direct opposition to
the mistake that was
indirectly taken.

Excerpts and passages from my
soul's interior
more than the intent behind
love
but aligned perpetually
with the very essence.

Acting silly...?

08.10.09

Never will I know that particular truth
lengthy pauses lose sight of the seconds
moments make in history.

Therefore, I come late in a past tense
realm of created realism,
where my beliefs lead me to believe that
I can be believed in.

Interpretations of insinuated injustices
are introduced by the one interpreting.
In that I rest. In that I breathe.
Knowing that no one will ever know
about me.

Never will I know that particular truth.
Move on I will have to, move on I would,
but I can't move.

      No leverage.

10.24.09

4,869 days in

Candidly pacifying mediocrity condemned in
yesterday's vengeance
External notes are positioned in the mountainous
regions where breathing stops.

Partially defeated firmly gripping a slightly
torn thread
Attached to everything unattainable,
so seduced by severity.

Confronted by the crushing blow of convictions,
covered in the silence, bearing no name.
Adorned with senseless ridicule,
but guilty of foolish participation.

Candidly pacifying mediocrity condemned in
yesterday's vengeance
For no other reason but for my very own
affinity to explore.
      This is the proof of purchase
            evidently unredeemable.

11.23.09

4,899 days in

An unseen enemy caught in
rapid motion disguised with
the air of shadows.
   Contained.
Withheld within movement yet extremely
enveloped amidst
routine.

Regulated progress, adapted
minds of wretchedness.
Relying so heavily upon
self-control as endurance
seems faulty under the
cloak of immovable
darkness.

Deliberate impurities are
dealt in mass quantity,
Ingested through weakness
and confined in disharmony.

My adversary is time,
   unrelenting and often unchangeable.

11.29.09

4,905 days in

    Elevated extremes sprinkle burnt rose petals
over a thin sheet of normalcy,
    While the stench of severed wishes smells appealing
almost when sadly considering the equivalent.

    Hidden dangers appear lucid,
        darkness rampant and light is withering away
        at the pace of a snail's future.

    Visualizations of success and triumph
        are choked and nailed by the hammer of despair,
        left in peril to be washed away on the shores
        of meandering evils.

    Aimless attacks of detachment have proven
to be most futile at best,
    The distorted plan rages on yet deterred by one
lasting entity.......tenacity.

2010

4,938 days in | 6,011 days to release

———

Place amidst the fabric of your heart something
that strengthens, soothes, and endures forever.

———

You never know how much you crave being treated like a human being until you're deprived of that feeling and then those feelings are restored through experience. So many years had slipped between my fingers, was I just doing time like everybody else and going through the motions? If you have nothing to gauge your change or evolution, it's hard to know if you've grown.

Growing up in the prison system had been a sour reality but it was my reality nonetheless, so face it I had to.

I had worked several job assignments in the 6th prison I was currently house in. I had been working in segregation passing out dinner trays when that deprivation I spoke of in the beginning got awakened.

I met an officer that worked in the control booth in segregation. We would discuss politics, sports, day to day stresses and child rearing because she was expecting a child. Oddly enough our connection was purely platonic. It felt good to communicate with someone who saw me as an adult male with ideas and opinions and not just as a prison number and barcode. Hell, maybe I was socially recognizable after all and not the latter.

This prison was dark for me and represented a depressing time, yet still a period in my life of transition. I had begun the second stage of my own rehabilitation and reform, it felt much better to let go of a lot of those things from the past; people included. It's not about forgetting, but about forgiving myself for allowing those things to rule me for so long.

As much as I'd like to say my writing felt therapeutic for me at times, in this instance having someone that wasn't a criminal confirm my humanity, felt great. It reaffirmed yet again, that I would make it.

01.16.10

4,953 days in

Much obliged to believe
in dreams unfulfilled
Weary treading over
sinking roads.

Love lives within.
Torn between romanticism
and cynicism.
To exist purposefully
is selfless love hidden
under perplexities.

Deep yearning.
Unquenched desires.
Sweet visions of embracing
softness as it gently
captures admiration.

That day is here,
It breathes in suffocation
and pulsates with vigor
even in the face of death.

05.19.10

Caressing,
    two vindicated souls exploring
        possibilities without limitations.

No thought of sin and consequence,
    no one's here to judge or
    criticize us...so, be yourself,
        free and untamed.

Be wise beyond others in what it is
    only you know what to do to me.

Your world and your rules,
    colorful and exaggerant
    but very much worthwhile.

You were made for love,
    made to be cherished
    made to be adored and to
    be catered to.

Believe that I was made to love you
    the way you desire and dream to
    be loved and it will be so.
Believe that I was made specifically
for your very own benefit,
    and it will be so.

Just believe.

09.05.10

5,185 days in

Emotional confessions frightened
and helpless.
Laced in negative attractions,
drowning in this worlds' sadness.

Quoted phrases of hate repeated
by winners who feel they are
defeated.
Drama jam-packed in every crevice
even upliftment begins to sound
like a destructive message.

Where do we go from here?
When love is estranged and trust
becomes fear.
Loneliness is in abundance,
joy has fallen short where pain
has grown triumphant.

Smiling hard enough to suffocate
the tears,
Using a watch to study the minutes
as I try to ignore the past years.

Laced in negative attractions,
smothered by this prison madness.

Black Mother

10.09.10 | 5,219 days in

This poem in particular was written after I watched a news broadcast highlighting a church in Southern Illinois. It was a predominantly Black church and so I saw an elderly black mother walking into the church. In that moment, I felt so responsible for all the pain I caused my own mother, grandmother and aunt. There I sat in prison with only my aunt Michelle left alive, so I wrote this piece for her and all the other women of color that we as black men have disgraced with our behavior. This poem is called Black Mother.

Black mother, the strength that honed and nurtured the quality of my leadership.

You ensured me of my importance in more ways than there are words that exist.

Perilous is your journey. Your crown has dust, it has dirt, and the saliva from my ignorant shouts smearing it.

Still, it is worn when most don't believe you deserve to be adorned in such a prestigious piece.

Black mother, please forgive my violent outbursts, my apocalyptic sized destruction of our indestructible yearning to be and remain as one.

I've adopted ways that should have never been mastered and physically displayed...for this I apologize.

My Black mother, I'll be forever fond of your tenacity. That's why I pray for the day when you accept my divine partnership again. For when we stood together our bond was ten times eternal.

Black mother of my offspring, please accept my faults as proof that mistakes create experience and wisdom. I LOVE YOU QUEEN! But maybe our future holds greatness unattainable in this particular century...I'll still keep trying.

10.27.10

5,237 days in

Two blinks separate us
from now
and eternity.
How foolish is our
attempt at arresting
moments that create
immortality?
Bright dreams fall
on deaf ears,
broken wishes mold
and contour themselves
into the shape of our
ambition.
Somber, desolate adults
traipse through this
life
embracing doubt,
marrying regret and
divorcing their true
realities.
Too bitter to see beyond
yesterday,
too naïve to enjoy
tomorrow.
Capturing moments of joy
for only two blinks.

Try not to look away.

12.14.10

5,285 days in

Prolific and painstaking,
unacknowledged missing component
with game changing elements.
Lucifer's whispers have turned
into screams.
Alluring aromas of greed.
Plucked from society's
flock of roaming sheep,
once roaming free
destined to be nothing
but a faded memory.
Moving at the same pace as
Dripping honey,
Way slower than those days
of fast money
it sounds a bit funny
Stale laughter
interrupted by a dry cough
"Shake a leg top bunk!"
a disturbing reminder of
gun-toting and selling
that junk
Mama didn't raise no punk!
Living dramatically within
an outside source,
The product of annihilations'
entity
or just an intelligent
corpse?

12.14.10

5,285 days in

Standing still
froze in amazement
paralyzed pupils dilated.
Lust is an intoxicating
battlefield
where less is more.
Incented ambiance.
Rapture incited melodies
bodies in synchronized
motion
bumping and bombarding
finding destinations without
a compass, map or GPS.
Only stopping after the
wordless lyrics have been
completed.
Tarnished techniques fail to be
critiqued.
The duo came together in unison
sounding and serenading like
a live band
emphasized admiration
reveling in justifiable
romantic fantasies.

    Will they be forgotten
        or lost in time
            like me?

2011

5,303 days in | 5,646 days to release

We can change anything in our lives that begins and exists solely as a thought first.

The definition of humility goes as follows: "the absence of any feelings of being better than others".

In my 7th prison, Big Muddy River Correctional Center, I found out what I was really made of when I began working I the Health Care Unit caring for terminally ill patients.

After working there for over a year I was introduced to a new patient that I would be looking after. The Physical Therapist told me about this new guy and she said that his arms didn't work anymore. "His arms don't work! Why?" I asked. She told me that he had ALS commonly known as Lou Gehrig's disease. ALS, or amyotrophic lateral sclerosis, is a progressive neurodegenerative disease that affects nerve cells in the brain and the spinal cord.

When I finally saw him, he was a white male maybe 6'2" if he was standing (he was in a wheelchair), and he had on a prison issued uniform with a thermal top on underneath. This was strange because it was the summer, so either he was anemic or ashamed of the new state of his arms.

He pretty much needed help with everything. Only two days there and the Head nurse decided it was time for his first bath. Of course it was my job to assist her by getting him in this huge harness that lowers patients into the bathtub. The nurse took his shirt off and all of his tattoos were shown and the majority of them were Aryan Brotherhood.

Shocked and appalled, I had to hide my obvious distaste. He had a noose on his arm that had the words, "White man's best friend" and a Swastika among others. It surely would have been easier to hate him with such controversial body art displayed in the open. Honestly though, I didn't know him as a person or know about the circumstances that lead him down the path to getting those tatts, nor did he know me, and if everybody has a story, I couldn't really judge him. As much as I wanted to, I couldn't.

In the months that passed I learned more about him and how he made those decisions he made to don such hateful tattoos. Illinois prison history would tell you that in the 1970's you had to choose your race in certain maximum security prisons or you would definitely become prey.

Me and this guy eventually became friends and I even joked with him saying how funny it was that Black Power was taking care of White Power, he laughed until he coughed.

During this time of my life I gained an insight, a tolerance and a greater appreciation for life. We underestimate one great truth 'cause we're too busy with our personal agendas and that is, we only have one life, and when it's gone, it's gone.

If I never valued what I said to people, or what my legacy would eventually be before then, I sure changed my tune after this experience. This was really and truly a year of humility.

08.15.11

5,529 days in

Left for ruin we are,
  separated by our own conceit.
Moments of selfish indulgence have
  squeezed the passion out of some.
Opportunity for change struggles,
  crippled by the constant reminder
  of who you once were.

Seeking...Grasping...the unknown can
  be very difficult to comprehend.
Pride torn to pieces from the choices
  made by lust,
when smiles lacked ulterior motive,
  negativity didn't have a voice.

Calendars pass in rapid succession.
  How would you feel if you were
  publicly ridiculed,
  banished beyond the shadows and
  seen by no one?

Imagining those rare occasions when
  you actually mattered,
  when you spoke and someone listened.
Now all you can do is place a stranglehold
  on your past memories.
    Trying not to lose them as well.

                Alone amongst thousands.

08.22.11

5,536 days in

Intense physical allure
I've become inebriated
inside the idea of her
sweet taste
caught in the rapture...drunkenness.

Thoughts frozen when we
lock eyes for the
briefness that a glance takes.

With words stumbling
over one another
it's a wonder I can even
speak at all.

Tell me for one second
that you will be mine,
maybe not entirely,
for such a woman I'm sure
is highly sought after,
if not taken.

Lie to me anyway,
make me believe I'll feel
this way forever,
knowing I won't.

Hanging on to your every word,
caught in the rapture...intoxicated.

Expecting what may never happen,
but still expecting.

10.27.11

Caught in time,
suspended in the middle
of nowhere and death.
 Surrounded.

Soothed by the dangerous
silence of my own pain,
how wonderful,
several losses created
one tremendous gain.

Openly conversing with
charismatic psychopaths,
socially awkward,
yet friends with everyone.

Caught in time,
suspended in the middle
of nowhere and death,
on the very cusp
of greatness,
but still lacking.

2012

5,668 days in | 5,281 days to release

Why hold onto something, someone, or a feeling
that causes pain and has no positive usefulness?

With nothing and no one outside of myself to prove that I have gotten better in decision making, what is my next move? Am I just a pawn inside the bigger plan of chessboard strategies designed to keep a certain demographic off the playing field and to continue lining the pockets of the prison industrial complex?

All I can say is "You're welcome" because I did assist in the current state of my prison existence. This is a road to travel and when I reach the end of it I'll still have a lot to talk about and reflect on. TIME MOVES FORWARD.

Having a serious relationship while doing a 60 year prison term is almost, if not, nonexistent. I've had love come into my life and ease so much pain, then, all of a sudden you wake up one day and never receive another letter again. A person can easily change their mind about being there for you when you're doing a lengthy sentence. Even your family can disappear when they feel like it.

Sometimes people will come back and act like they weren't gone for 5 or even 10 years, but I guess where I am I should just accept whoever comes into my life and be grateful. At least this is what it sounds like and feel like to us serving time.

A lot of us in here need a good support system, not just financially, but mentally. This would mark my 16th year in prison and my maturity, problem solving skills and my ability to hold a decent conversation was all by my own choice to evolve.

My patient with the ALS passed away in June of this year and that was something because I felt bad for how he went out and didn't have a chance to do it all better than before. I got shipped to another facility called Shawnee Correctional Center, and it was located 15 minutes from Kentucky.

Initially, I did not like being moved to that place, but I started taking some cognitive behavioral classes to gain more insight into who I was at that point.

I had to write this a paper for this class and it fell into the Head Counselor's hands. She liked the material and would eventually use parts of my paper for the class graduation. This chance meeting turned into an interview to become a Peer Presenter for the prison. I began the orientation process and was taught to present for the class called TRAC-1 which stood for Trained. Ready. And. Capable.

It was during this time when I learned that I was a natural at using my story to help others in the same situation. Seeing my positive effect on people made me realize that I could be a motivational speaker upon release if I wanted to. In the middle of one of the most racist prisons in Illinois, I found yet another part of my strength. I couldn't let my old self determine the fabric of my future.

"Love conquers all", is what I've always heard so I'll have to love myself enough to make it, and eventually make something of myself. Time never stops, no matter what's happening in your life or what stage of your development you're in.

02.07.12

5,705 days in

Spontaneous exhilaration,
in pursuit of seemingly
unattainable happiness.
Evidence of previous
failures rest in the eyes
of the heartbroken,
while fortified structures
are erected to oppose
what could possibly change
everything.
Captured so effectively
without warning,
second-guessed and afraid of
the unknown.
Letting it all slip away
is realistic,
for pain is more appealing than
happiness and love.
    Or so it seems.

07.13.12

5,862 days in

Wishing that I could've said more,
    openly pursuing your heart and soul
        with unrelenting purpose.
Circumstances and timing has a nasty
    way of placing unwarranted gag orders
        on romantic exploration.

Despite my efforts, the opportunity
    never appeared where I could tell
        you that you were more than you
           thought,
for by fate had it, who knows where
    our hearts would have travelled
        past that first glance?

Maybe the multiple mazes and scattered
    paths of life will steer us
        back into one another's presence.
If that too is an overly fabricated
    fantasy of my own making,
        be assured that my memories of you
        will be undiminished by time
        and distance,
    but moreso grasped in a strong
        embrace and kept peacefully
        in the everlasting caverns
        of my spirit.

2013

6,034 days in | 4,915 days to release

Fear is what stops us from doing a lot, saying a lot and being a lot more than we can be.

Sometimes we stifle our own growth by being scared of the unknown, especially when familiarity breeds complacency. I remembered how I spent my first year in a max joint. I sat by the door of the cell and listened intently to my surroundings. A lot of the men I paid close attention to had been in prison since the late "70's" or the early "80's". I made a point of watching them and listening to them because I had to do 30 straight years before I could be released.

As I worked out with them and made meals with them I learned something very real and astonishing. These men were mostly worn down and bitter due to the time away from the free world. Their people skills were gone and the level of maturity didn't match their respective age groups. I didn't like it, hearing ignorance and sorrow all the time bothered me.

I devoted myself to reading books that taught human nature and self-help material and sometime relationship books on marriage and raising children. The best thing I ever studied in prison was the study of "me". We have to take an objective look at ourselves before we can start this process. The hardest thing to do is to have a thug take responsibility for his overall actions without blaming someone else.

This is a place where the same guilt that got you here, is the one thing that makes people apathetic to your plights while doing and facing the time. If you got yourself in this position, then you knew what you would have to face in the long run. There is no truth to this at all. I didn't know that the bulk of my immediate family would pass away while I was in prison. The things that I have learned and felt during this prison term could have never been predicted in any way.

Although it was my 17th year in prison it was still a tug of war mentally, to change amidst the unwarranted destructive thoughts of others, to wake up happy surrounded by misery and to foolishly make plans when others controlled the better part of your day. The anxiety of being somewhere you wish you were not, has the sustaining power to cripple any creative juices from flowing.

You are alone with the "REAL" you and all the failures that created the flawed blueprint and roadmap that lead you to where you are. A stark realization of this magnitude doesn't exist for most inmates because it begins with responsibility for wrong action and the ultimate knowledge of self.

At this point I had fully changed and knew without a doubt that I would never commit another crime. I filed a Nunc Pro Tunc *(English translation: "now for then" is a Latin expression in common legal use in the United States, the United Kingdom, and other countries. In general, a ruling nunc pro tunc applies retroactively to correct an earlier ruling.)* in Circuit Court to correct an error at my sentencing that had the potential of knocking off 4 years. I needed this because I didn't know how much more growth could be done in this place. I think being tested is what polishes greatness and I just hope at the end of all this I can turn out to be great.

02.06.13

6,070 days in

Wrath of my sinful past,
        dark cloud circulating.
Years tear through the once
        impenetrable fortress
            that loyalty constructed.

Whatever is left after the
        broken dreams and shattered
            wishes,
        please take it somewhere
            and nurture the remnants.

If tears could save someone
        from any future pain I'd
        have an eternity of happiness
            to cherish,
still laughed at for my merits,
        but refusing to be
        categorized by the separation
            of my parents.

Know me and not of me,
        do your best not to think
        that you're above me,
maybe then we can begin as friends,
        you might find out that
            you love me.

        An authentic wish.

02.12.2013

6,076 days in

The only architect with
obvious limitations.
Portraits painted in
private have flaws too.

Basic theories that
become complex
places me amongst
familiar faces,
undermined by my own
assessment.

In fear of what never was,
feeling confident about
what may never be.
Empty desires harmonize
with deceiving appearances.

Impersonated enjoyment.

2015

6,764 days in | 4,185 days to release

———

Live by those same moralities in which you would wish
your dying legacy to be remembered.
Honor your life.

———

Last year was the hardest one to date. My Aunt Michelle passed away. She raised me, sacrificed so much of her own life to make sure I knew that I was loved and could be whatever I wanted to be. Without her, I had no one left, at least in my opinion. My Uncle Bobby was all the way in Germany and we only spoke to one another when someone died, our relationship needed to be healed drastically.

Finding a way to move forward and remain strong the way my 3 Queens taught me, I met the woman who would eventually become my wife and best friend. As strong as I was, I still had pain in my life. I still had a long way to go on my sentence and I had really fallen in love this time...it was change-your-life real.

I was transferred to my 9th facility called Dixon Correctional Center and I was also reunited with guys that I had started this time with almost 20 years prior.

Things were moving in a seemingly positive direction when I saw in the news that a white man went into a black church in the south and killed 9 people. It prompted me to write the only poem I penned in pure rage. Hate still existed out there and I had to understand that, live with it, and find a way to be positive about my eventual release back into what seems to be the same madness I left 2 decades ago.

Time will tell how this story plays itself out.

06.18.2015

6,932 days in

The good die young.

> By whose implication does such an
>> embellishment bear truth?
> Widespread urban genocide based
>> solely on petty animosities
>> derived from antiquated beliefs.

> From where was your distaste for me created?

> The last words of a dying man.
>> Another victim of senseless brutality.
>> Savagery without provocation.

> The excessive onslaught continues to
>> touch every square mile of the
>> Earth's surface.
> Amplified by all media outlets
>> and glorified by an easily
>> swayed society.
> A bloodthirst seemingly unquenchable.

> Innocent lives are ruined on both sides,
>> offspring left with no physical
>> image to parallel their likeness.

> Why does it always end in blood and cruelty?

> Chaos, calamity and disorder has found
>> away to trump peace and harmony yet again.

> Violence,
>> the source of its origin pales in comparison
>> to its everlasting impact.

Broken ideals.

Author's Closing Remarks

I leave you with this:

Sometimes I have cried inside without even shedding one tear, but the circumstances of this reality remain the same.

The sight of visualized tears cannot change this experience. I must understand the message life is telling me and make positive advancements amongst the pain of what is.

I've been turned around, unaccepted and almost mentally broken, showered in love on occasion and other times I was misused, mistreated and forgotten.

At times I've been known for nothing, and others highly remembered for everything. Exceeding my own expectations of expecting more than I should expect.

Maybe I just see all the theatrics of a silver lining when I don't have the fabric to design the garment.

Wrapping myself in the warmth of my...withheld ambition.

A. M. Walker

Pain*

March 8, 2018 | 7926 Days in

I…Pledge allegiance to the pain, while mouthing a solemn
oath to whatever surviving strands of my sanity that remains,
the stain on my heart has no filter as my thoughts never
have, I cried so many times within 22 years, the people that
left me in prison assume I never laugh- my better
half…attempts consoling me but parole for me is smothering
with all of its supervisory-laced restrictions, based on prior
convictions I'm teeter-tottering between success, failure,
picking that pole back up or having a smooth transition
borderline losing my religion, I…I pledge allegiance to the
pain, withheld ambition boiling in my veins
by the grace of the Creator I'm still composed
rose petal scented footsteps cold
I'm the descendant of the same King in Kemet Kush that lost
his nose…Pain.
Now where I came from, they treat hittas like royalty, and for
a bigger piece of the pie your best friend will shoot you in the
eye and peel off singing, "Loyalty, loyalty, loyalty".
It's hard to be humble when you're the lion that conquered
the jungle,
positive forward progress is heavily scrutinized, personal
haters and family members are the only one patiently waiting
on you to fumble, yet before I cower and before I crumble,
I…pledge allegiance to the pain…while mouthing a solemn
oath to whatever surviving strands of my sanity that remains.

*Pain is from "Sikiliza: A Visual Diary " – the second book of
poetry that Anthony is currently writing.

Anthony M. Walker

Anthony grew up on the West Side of Chicago as an only child. An array of bad choices led him down the wrong path. Anthony was in jail at 19 and sentenced to 60 years all before the age of 23. This is only part of where his story begins.

Facing 30 consecutive years of imprisonment, Anthony used his pen and paper as therapy to heal the wounds of his past. As a humble student of the human condition, he became a Peer Presenter and always maintained a positive attitude despite the fact of where he was.

Anthony's poems take you inside the prison journey of a young man on the road to his manhood and desperately chasing redemption.

A creative force, he is a fitness enthusiast, an innovator, an aspiring motivational speaker, and a person with strong entrepreneurial drive.

Anthony is currently working on, "Sikaliza: A visual Diary", which will be his second book of poetry. He makes the most of every single day by staying active, keeping a forward thinking attitude and he's always singing and dancing.